DR.STOXX

Since 2002

The Dr. Stoxx Complete Day-Trading Course

How to Trade for Extra Income

The Dr. Stoxx Complete Day-Trading Course

How to Trade for Extra Income

Happy Trading!

Dr. Thomas K. Carr, M.Phil., D.Phil. (Oxon.)

©2016 Befriend the Trend Publishing

ISBN-13:
978-0692611388 (Befriend the Trend Publishing)

ISBN-10:
069261138X

About Dr. Thomas Carr and DrStoxx.com

Dr. Carr has been actively trading the markets since 1996 following several years of studying technical analysis. He has been interviewed by the *Wall Street Journal* and *US News and World Report* for his insights into trading psychology. He is the author of the international bestseller, *Trend Trading for a Living* (McGraw-Hill, 2004), along with two other McGraw-Hill books on trading.

In 2002, Dr. Carr launched DrStoxx.com, a one-stop-shop for active traders. Today DrStoxx.com offers 5 market letters – including the hugely successful *Momentum Letter* – trading manuals, webinars and a managed accounts service. In 2015, Dr. Carr launched a companion site for long-term investors which publishes The IXTHYS Letter (ixthysletter.com). The *Dr. Stoxx Options Letter* is available through Marketfy.com. The *Dr. Stoxx Options Letter* is currently ranked as Marketfy's #1 most profitable market advisory.

About Befriend the Trend Publishing

Befriend the Trend Publishing is a subsidiary of Befriend the Trend Trading, LLC, a limited liability company founded in October, 2002, to serve the needs of active traders. Its mission is to provide active traders with high quality, easy to understand trading systems and trader training in books and manuals like this one.

Dr. Carr's "Learn to Trade" Resources Available on Amazon.com and DrStoxx.com:

- How to Make 50% per Month Trading Stocks
- The All-New Mean Reversion System
- The Dr. Stoxx Options Trading Manual
- Momentum Trading!

Dr. Carr's Market Letters Available on DrStoxx.com and Marketfy.com

- The Trend Trade Letter
- The Cheap Stocks Letter
- The ETF Trend Letter
- The ETF Weekly Index Letter
- The Momentum Letter
- The Dr. Stoxx Options Letter (#1 Letter on Marketfy!)

Dr. Carr's Managed Accounts service:

- Available June, 2016
- Register your interest at www.drstoxx.com

Contents

1. What is Day-Trading?
   a. What Day-trading Is and Is Not
   b. Advantages of Day-trading
   c. PDT Rules: How to Day-trade with a Small Account
   d. Being in the Right Frame of Mind

2. What You Need to Get Started
   a. Hardware
   b. Charting Services
   c. Online Brokers
   d. Starting Capital and Position Size

3. Setting Up Your Watch List
   a. Create Your Primary Watch List
   b. Set up Your Charting Workstation
   c. Becoming a Tape Reader
   d. How to Train Your Tape Reading Intuition

4. Five Day-Trading Systems
   a. Know your Candlesticks
   b. System 1: Countertrend Gap Down
   c. System 2: Countertrend Gap Up
   d. System 3: The Bullish MA-Tag
   e. System 4: The Bearish MA-Tag
   f. System 5: The Long/Short Mac-Stoch System

5. A Final Word

1. WHAT IS DAY-TRADING?

First of all, let me congratulate you, good purchaser of this Befriend the Trend Trading Manual, for taking the first step toward becoming an independent trader. Whether you bought this manual to learn how to trade by yourself and for yourself, or whether you bought it simply to help you make better decisions as you follow one or more of the DrStoxx.com market letters, your decision to educate yourself on the logistics of trading is a big step toward establishing your ultimate financial independence. You have opted for a more active role in your trading experience, and that alone is to be applauded. It was a manual much like this one you are now reading that launched me on my career as a trader, and I hope this publication does something similar for you as well.

You have chosen The Dr. Stoxx Complete Day-trading Course, which means that you are interested in learning how to maximize your trading profits by entering and exiting your trades within the same trading day. In this first section, we are going to define what Day-trading is, and what advantages Day-trading has for the individual trader.

What Day-trading Is and Is Not

It is essential to think of Day-trading, or DT as we'll call it from here on, as merely one form of short-term trading similar to other forms. It follows the same rules and setups used by other short-term traders. It scans for the same technical setups, looks for the same price patterns, anticipates the same breakout moves, and uses the same support and resistance techniques. There are only two things that distinguish day-trading as unique: it relies almost exclusively on intraday charts (typically the 5min. chart) instead of daily and weekly charts, and in no case is a DT position held overnight.

DT is perhaps best understood by contrast to other forms of online trading. Further clarification of the different types of trading styles can be defined as follows:

- **Buy-and-hold Investing**

  - AIM: long-term capital gains
  - STYLE: fundamental analysis of sectors and companies
  - HOLDING TIME: 1 year or longer
  - TIME INVESTMENT: a few hours each month
  - TURNOVER RATE: 5 to 10 trades per year
  - COMMISSION COSTS: minimal
  - EXPECTED ANNUAL RETURN: +15% or more

- **Position Trading**

  - AIM: quarterly income
  - STYLE: technical analysis of weekly/daily charts
  - HOLDING TIME: 20 to 100 trading days
  - TIME INVESTMENT: a few hours each week
  - TURNOVER RATE: 5 to 10 trades per month
  - COMMISSION COSTS: moderately low
  - EXPECTED ANNUAL RETURN: +25% or more

- **Swing Trading**

  - AIM: monthly income
  - STYLE: technical analysis of daily/hourly charts
  - HOLDING TIME: 2 to 20 trading days
  - TIME INVESTMENT: 2+ hours each day
  - TURNOVER RATE: 5 to 10 trades per week
  - COMMISSION COSTS: moderately high
  - EXPECTED ANNUAL RETURN: +40% or more

- ***Day Trading***

  - *AIM: weekly income*
  - *STYLE: technical analysis of intraday charts*
  - *HOLDING TIME: minutes to hours, 1 day maximum*
  - *TIME INVESTMENT: 5+ hours each day*
  - *TURNOVER RATE: 5 or more trades per day*
  - *COMMISSION COSTS: very high*
  - *EXPECTED ANNUAL RETURN: +50% or more*

On a percentage basis, the expected gains from any single day-trade are minimal relative to longer-term holds. This is due to the short holding period: a stock can only move so much in a day. An ideal day-trade gain is anything over 1.0% net return on equity. In a $50 stock, for example, this would amount to a modest $0.50 gain per share. Most day-trading gains are smaller than that. But this reduction of gain is offset by larger position sizing (which means you'll need a larger account size if you want to day-trade) and a high number of daily trades placed that are requirements of any DT strategy.

Total average gain per trade for a robust DT system, not including covering the spread (the amount between bid and ask), commissions, margin expenses, and losses, is normally in the +0.1% to +0.2% range, and the winning percentage on all trades usually hovers in the mid-60's. While buy-and-holders, position traders and swing traders will normally put 10% or less of their total account into each trade, day-traders put as much as 50% of the total cash in their account into each trade, using margin frequently ("margin" is money you borrow from your broker, at interest, to trade with) to leverage that size. As long as a position is not held overnight, losing trades are quickly closed, and winners are allowed to run into the close, this use of margin is appropriate.

So how much money can one make day-trading? That depends, of course, on how large your trading account is, how robust your trading system is, and how well you execute its rules. But to give you a benchmark, let's use some typical numbers.

If you have $100,000 in your account...

...and you make an average gain of +0.15% per trade (which is close to average for a robust system well traded)...

...and you place 5 trades per day with 40% of your account ($40,000) in each trade, using margin to cover the times you are more than 100% invested...

You will make a gross return of:

- $300 per day, or
- $1,500 per week, or
- $6,450 per month, or
- $77,400 per year.

Once you factor out trading costs – slippage, commissions, margin expenses – you'll come pretty close to the 50% net annual gain which is the ideal expectation of the day-trader. Of course, this does not includes taxes. Keep in mind that taxes on any trade held less than one year are at the same rate as your income tax bracket. For some this can mean a tax bill of 35% or more.

Given all that, and given that in certain market conditions (flat, choppy or non-trending markets) intraday stock movements can be reduced thus reducing overall day-trading gains, you can quickly see that to day-trade for a living requires a substantial account size. Thus it is most realistic to think of day-trading as a great way to supplement your income. If you can spend a couple hours trading each day with a $50,000 trading account, you can $100 to $200 a day to your bottom line. This quickly adds up. While it may be a number of years before you can support a family by trading, in the meantime you can use your trading proceeds (after setting aside funds for giving and taxes) to do some fun things with your finances.

Advantages of Day-trading

Again, while the net percentage gains of DT may be small, the overall returns can be huge because of the high number of trades made, the short holding period, and the large position sizing. To get an idea of what can be achieved through day-trading, read this story of Dan Zanger, published by Forbes magazine on December 18th, 2000:

My Stocks Are Up 10,000%!

Dan Zanger

By Lee Clifford

Every few weeks last fall, a shifting array of Dan Zanger's friends would gather in the basement of his Los Angeles home. They weren't there for chitchat, however, or to watch the game. They were there to witness a performance--and to learn.

For a few hours at a time, anywhere from three to five buddies would sit rapt in the darkened room, with windows shuttered to keep out the light, trying to glean the secrets of an artist at work. His blond hair as rumpled as his casual clothes, Zanger sat in front of five computer screens like a rock keyboardist surrounded by synthesizers. His body would tense as his eyes darted over the scrolling list of 800 stocks that he follows. Every so often, with the flick of a finger, he'd enter a buy or sell order.

Zanger would concentrate so hard that he didn't notice when spectators came and went. He wouldn't hear the questions they called to him. "I'm like a surgeon going in to do an operation," says Zanger. "I'm totally focused."

It's no wonder his friends and neighbors were curious. Just three years ago, Zanger, 47, was paying his bills by working in Beverly Hills as a swimming pool contractor, building Hefner-worthy tropical fantasy pools for rich and famous clients. In a good year he could make $50,000. Since then his investing, Zanger says, has turned $11,000 in savings into $18 million. That's a gain of 164,000%. "As far as I know," he exults, "it's the world record."

Talk about any recent investing trend, and Zanger will tell you he was one step ahead of the market. "I foretold the biotech move two or three months ahead of time," he says. And those other investors who got whipsawed by the rapid turnaround in Internet stocks? Not Zanger. He says he was short-selling those stocks. Referring to a prediction he made in an investing newsletter that he began publishing last year, Zanger adds, "I showed everybody the market top of March 10."

Yeah, yeah, yeah. We've all met a Dan Zanger--or 20. You know whom we're talking about: the guy at work who won't shut up about how he's whipping every fund manager on the planet with his tech portfolio. The golf buddy who can't stop droning on about the excruciatingly obscure--but incredibly lucrative--options scenarios he picked up from a $25 book. Or your neighbor's 21-year-old kid who, to hear his parents tell it, has made enough in the market to pay for their retirement.

The only difference? Zanger appears to be telling the truth. His 1999 tax return and trading records, which he shared with FORTUNE, show capital gains of $14,232,878.

Zanger is rare, but he's not alone. We undertook to locate members of a very unusual breed: individual investors who chalked up out-of-the-ballpark returns-- and were willing to prove it with tax or trading records. Though no one was able to equal Zanger's universe-beating numbers, we did find a tiny, scattered tribe of investors with the kind of results that entitle them to all the cocktail-party bragging they want to indulge in. Our not-so-motley selection includes everyone from a stay-at-home dad to a personal trainer. Their investing styles couldn't be more different, though they usually combine an Olympian tolerance for risk with a penchant for unorthodox strategies that involve charts, options, margin, and the like--not to mention insane luck. They all have one thing in common: They are hands-down, no two ways about it, making mincemeat out of all those highly paid pros.

By definition, most of us can't beat the market averages. But since investing became America's most popular participatory sport in the '90s, outperforming Wall Street wisemen has become a national obsession. It's the quintessential American myth--Anybody can make it big--reincarnated for the new millennium. And like any compelling myth, it requires a handful of unlikely individuals to keep us convinced that, yes, a muscle-bound personal trainer can outinvest a hedge-fund manager with billions of dollars in his portfolio. It's a tale Horatio Alger might have penned--if he had known a world with discount brokers and online investing.

So what's Zanger's secret? The former pool contractor, who resembles a poor man's--er, a rich man's--Richard Branson, was always more than happy to explain his secrets to his friends once the market closed. He would become animated, describing to his awed flock why he bought, say, 1,000 shares of

AskJeeves.com at the precise moment he did. The stock, he'd tell them, was clearly headed into a "pennant" formation--it had risen and then tapered off quickly--and thus seemed primed for another quick, steep increase.

His friends would look on in glassy-eyed bewilderment as he explained his "technical" investing philosophy. It's not exactly a strategy that would make Warren Buffett proud. Zanger completely ignores yardsticks such as price-earnings ratios and revenue growth. The only thing he cares about is how a stock is behaving. "I trade whatever the market is going to push up the most," Zanger says. "It doesn't matter what the company does, or what their earnings are." Devotees of technical analysis believe that stock prices move in easily recognizable visual patterns that an experienced investor can capitalize on. So when CMGI is gearing up to a "cup and handle," or Amazon is perilously close to a "descending triangle," or--egad--"channel formation," Zanger moves. He internalizes those curves, those spikes, like a doctor scrutinizing a heart patient's monitor in an intensive-care unit. "Stocks are my buddies," Zanger says. "I know when they feel good or when they feel bad." ...

This spring, Zanger says, he moved most of his assets into cash, shielding him from the tech meltdown. There the money will remain until his charts tell him the worst is over. While he waits for that to happen, Zanger is busy preparing to raze the home he recently bought in Kirkland, Wash. He plans to replace it with a dwelling modeled on Frank Lloyd Wright's Falling Water. "You should see the pool it's going to have," he swoons. As for the building of his mini-empire, Zanger is unequivocal: "It's the greatest story ever told."

Dan Zanger's experience is exceptionally rare. Keep in mind that he was trading during the most volatile and most bullish market in history. It is virtually impossible that anyone in today's less exuberant markets can make a sustained 10,000% annual return day-trading stocks. But it does go to illustrate what is possible in DT.

In addition to the possibility of high returns, DT has the added advantage of ATM-like income. Since you are in and out of the market on a daily basis, "banking" your profits at the end of each trading day, 100% "in cash" by 4 pm, EST, you have the opportunity to see your income accumulate on a daily basis. Unlike the longer-term trading strategies where you have to hold positions for weeks or even months, suffering through drawdowns as your stocks rise and fall with market dynamics, the positional drawdowns of a day-trader last for minutes, maybe an hour at most. By the end of the day, on most days, your account has posted a gain and your net worth as an individual trader has moved to the next level.

Another advantage of DT is related to the one just described. Since you are fully in cash between market sessions, you have absolutely no need to worry how overnight news will affect the markets while the markets are closed. A dip in commodity or currency futures, a selloff in the European markets, a terrorist attack, earnings announcements, upgrades and downgrades: none of these things can be causes for worry if you are out of the market overnight. As a day-trader, you react to unexpected market moves; you are not at their mercy. During the trading day, one can minimize risk by setting a stop loss on the trade. But overnight this is impossible. So DT is the best form of trading for those who, like many traders (including Dr Stoxx!), suffer from "trading-induced insomnia".

You can also work DT around your daily schedule. Some active day-traders only trade the morning hours. Others find an hour or two at lunchtime to trade. Still others trade only the closing hour. Those who day-trade the forex markets can trade in the evenings and early mornings, outside of the more limited stock market hours. While part-time DT is not as profitable as fulltime trading, it is nevertheless something that can be done by the working professional.

The PDT Rule: How to Day-trade with a Small Account

Day-traders rapidly buy and sell stocks throughout the day in the hope that their stocks will continue climbing or falling in value for the minutes to hours they own the stock, allowing them to lock in quick profits. DT can be both extremely profitable and extremely risky and can result in substantial financial losses in a very short period of time.

This is why, before a U.S. Senate subcommittee, former SEC Chairman Arthur Levitt testified that, "I am concerned that some day traders don't fully understand the level of risk they are assuming. I am concerned that some people may be lured into the false belief that day-trading is a surefire strategy to make them rich."

With these concerns in mind, on February 27, 2001, the Securities and Exchange Commission (SEC) approved rule changes proposed by the New York Stock Exchange (NYSE) and the National Association of Securities Dealers (NASD) aimed at imposing more stringent margin requirements for day-trading customers. Under these rules, customers who are deemed "pattern day-traders" (PDT's) must have at least $25,000 in their accounts and can only trade in margin accounts. A "pattern day-trader" is a trader who executes more than two day-trades in any given week. If a trader with less than $25,000 in his or her account executes more than 2 day-trades in any given 5-trading-day period, that account is closed to all new positions until a 5-day period is cleared with 2 or fewer day-trades in it.

What in effect the PDT ruling has done is to virtually eliminate day-trading as a possibility for those who are most in need of it: the smaller account trader. Those with larger accounts can afford to weather the downturns of longer-term holds, the smaller trader cannot.

But there are a couple of ways around these "PDT" rules the SEC has imposed on under-capitalized traders. One way is to trade using an "over-night trading" strategy that I outline in another of my Trading Manuals (*OverNightTrading*™). This is a form of day-trading in which the position is held for four distinct time periods: the last couple hours of trading, the after-hours session, the pre-market session, and the first hour of the day after entry. Because of the possibility of overnight gaps, it is riskier than day-trading, but this strategy tends to have a higher winning percentage than day-trading due to the longer holding period.

The other way of skirting the PDT rules is to realize that the rule only applies to stocks and stock options. You may therefore day-trade other non-equity based securities like forex (foreign exchange currency pairs), options on indexes and commodities, and the E-mini futures. Single Stock Futures, where they are still offered, are another option for PDT traders but they are now so thinly traded that their use in day-trading is limited.

One advantage to the single stock futures is that they operate on a 5:1 margin. This means that if it would have cost you $5,000 to buy 1 round lot of a $50 stock, it will only cost you $1,000 to buy in at the same investment level (1 contract) in the SSF. Thus if the stock moves 10% in your favor (to $55.00), your SSF investment is now worth $1,500, or a 50% increase! This leverage makes the SSF a very attractive day-trading vehicle. But again, they have fallen into such disuse that it is difficult finding contracts that have decent spreads (the distance between bid and ask). The single stock futures on SPY and QQQ tend to be the most heavily traded.

Another way to avoid the SEC penalty and still remain active as a day-trader is to trade the E-mini contracts. These are futures contracts, designed for smaller account traders (hence the name "mini"), on the Nasdaq 100, the S&P100, the Dow 30, the Russell 2000, the 10-year treasuries, among other underlying securities. I outline several effective and profitable methods for trading the E-minis in another Trading Manual (*The Dr. Stoxx Complete E-Mini Trading Course*), so we will withhold any comment on them here. The same is true with forex. In the near future I will have a complete course on forex trading available to you.

Having the Right Mindset

In order to profit regularly from DT, you need to have the right frame of mind going into the trade. It is essential to think of these trades as "1 day trades"; in no case are you going to hold overnight. You may think your position is going to skyrocket the next day, but there is no guarantee of that. Your mental approach going into each trade must be to cling lightly to your position, and be ready to exit quickly on clear signs of the trade going against you.

It is also important, as a balance, that you keep in mind that the stock you are in was specially chosen for its strong likelihood of trading favorably beyond your entry price at some point during the trading day. If you follow the methods we outline below, about 95% of the time you will be given an opportunity sometime during that day to take a profit on your position, however small. This can give you the confidence to hold on to those small drawdowns that inevitably come with day-trading (note that drawdowns come with the territory in any form of trading).

Holding these two competing ideas in balance is the key to successful DT. On the one hand, you need the quick reflexes and impulsive nature of a floor trader, and on the other hand, the steady confidence of a buy-and-hold investor. If you are too quick on the trigger, you will lose out on the many times your position makes great gains later in the day. But if you hold on too long, you may either see a decent profit turn into a loss, or a small loss become a much larger one.

Another "balanced" attitude you must possess as a day-trader is that between being bullish and being bearish. As an investor, position trader or swing trader, you must come into each trading day with a strong sense of where you see the market heading over the next few days, weeks, months or even years. But a day-trader cannot afford to have such a predisposition. "Directional bias" is the day-trader's downfall. Each trading day must be viewed through a *tabula rasa*, a blank slate that will be filled in as the day's activity unfolds. You should be equally as willing to take a short position (or stand aside if you do not take short positions) as a long position in any given hour during the trading day. In this Manual, I will teach you four proven DT systems, each with a long and short component. Willing to go either long or short at any time on any day is the proper attitude you must cling to.

For all these reasons, DT will test your trading skills like no other trading approach can. But fret not! We have ways of putting *100% mechanical* parameters on your position that will virtually eliminate 90% of the errors beginning day-traders make. These parameters will be described in detail below.

So with that as introduction, let's get started on the exciting, highly profitable adventure of DT!

2. WHAT YOU NEED TO GET STARTED

Hardware

I recommend using a recent model desktop PC computer. Any Windows-based desktop is the best choice for day-trading since most of the higher end software that is useful for short-term trading is only available in that format. The faster the processor speed the better. RAM should be maxed out in the machine. Load it up with as much as it will handle. In fact, RAM is more important than CPU speed. With a large amount of access memory, you will be able to run the high demand software necessary to trade properly all at once, without running the risk of "freezing" your machine due to overload. A terabyte sized hard drive is also a plus. You won't be storing things like videos and games on your trading computer, hopefully, but some of the software you need to day-trade can be space intensive.

The monitor is also an important piece of your trading arsenal. As a rule, the larger the monitor the better. For this reason, laptops are not the best choice for day-trading. They are fine for traveling purposes, but try opening your trading account platform, your real- time charts, a Time and Sales window, your watch lists, and an internet browser all at once and you will soon realize how necessary it is to have as much desktop space as possible. I use two huge monitors to trade from, and if you can afford it, I recommend this option. You may need to install a dual video card to handle more than one monitor, but the small investment will be worth it.

Charting Service

In order to day-trade profitably, you will need to use a high-end, premium charting service. This service will need to have the ability to save watch lists of up to 50 stocks each. The package should have all the standard technical indicators which can be displayed simultaneously (some lower end packages restrict you to viewing only one indicator at a time), real-time Time and Sales, Level II (though this is not necessary to trade the systems I teach here), and a data feed that includes forex and the e-mini futures contracts on the major indexes, if you wish to trade those.

The charting service you choose should be easy to read and user-friendly. The service packages I recommend and use myself are available from Metastock and eSignal. I am partnered with both companies and fully endorse their services.

If you need to cut overhead costs, you can use TradingView.com. It is a free, web-based charting service with real-time data, watch lists, and a full package of technical indicators. TradingView lacks time and sales data, however, and the chart updates using free data (via the BATS exchange) can be a bit buggy (i.e., slow to refresh). You get what you pay for! You can upgrade to a higher-end data package for about $10 per month plus additional exchange fees, however, which will give you a smoother end-user experience since the data feed is direct and not mediated. TradingView also has forex, e-mini and futures charts too but again, you will need to upgrade to get the best quality data. TradingView is my go-to service when I'm in a hurry or trading on my laptop from a hotel or airport. And did I mention, it's free?

Another site you will want to be familiar with is Finviz.com. I use Finviz for creating and building my watch lists of stocks. It is super easy to use, very fast, has all the pertinent data I need, a cool (though somewhat limited) back-testing feature for technical systems (which is very rare to find), updates in real-time, and full-featured technical charts. You'll want to upgrade to Finviz Elite, which only costs about $25/month as of this writing.

Online Brokers

I will just say a quick word about your online broker: you need one, a good one, an inexpensive one, and one whose online platform (and whose mobile platform, too) for inputting trades you are comfortable with and find easy to use. In the past I've used most of the popular online brokerages: E*Trade, Scottrade, Investrade, MB Trading, Schwab. All offer discount pricing and user-friendly trading systems. Currently I have my accounts with Interactive Brokers and would recommend them to anyone. I have found them to be reliable, inexpensive ($0.50 per 100 shares traded), with the lowest margin rates in the industry, the most extensive inventory of shares to short (and when they are out of shares, they go into the market and get them for you), and their account management system is fairly user-friendly. I also give them props for having improved their customer service tremendously over the years. Some people, however, find their "Trader Workstation", which is where you input your trades, cumbersome and confusing.

Starting Capital and Position Size

For reasons stated above – namely, the PDT rules – you will need to begin your DT career with at least $25,000 in your trading account. Because the learning curve is steep, and because that curve will cost you money, a more realistic starting amount is $30,000. If you start with $25,000, it will only take one loss to put you in violation of the PDT rules and therefore out of business for a week. With $30,000 you have a nice $5,000 cushion to absorb the inevitable mistakes of your initial efforts at day-trading.

You also want to make sure you have a *margin* account set up, not a *cash* account. Only in a margin account can you sell stocks short. With a cash account, shorting is not allowed. For the same reason, you cannot day-trade a tax-deferred retirement account. Also, a margin account allows you to borrow the broker's cash (normally up to 100% of your account value) for a small interest fee so that you can leverage your DT positions. Since DT aims at very small gains per trade, leveraging those gains is important.

So with $30,000 in your account, you will want to think of dividing your capital into equal lots and putting the same amount of cash into each position. If you are an experienced day-trader, using up to full margin (so, $60,000) and dividing that amount into 10 equal lots of $6,000 each is a good starting point for using the systems I teach in this Manual. If you are just starting your DT career, I would suggest beginning with about half that amount ($3,000 per trade). As long as you are paying a half penny per share in commission, you'll be able to turn a profit with that size. It may be only $3 or $4 per trade, but you'll be gaining experience, maintaining your capital, and learning what kind of trading best fits your trading style without running the risk of falling below the PDT standard.

There are tens of thousands of listed and over-the-counter stocks available for trading daily. It is impossible to monitor the whole universe of trading vehicles on a daily basis. So the logical thing to do, and what day-traders must do before they do anything else, is create and regularly update watch lists of stocks that meet certain criteria.

Some charting services will offer screening tools for subscribers, but for our purposes the free stock screener offered by Finviz.com (see description above) are all we need.

Create Your Primary Watch List

I recommend setting up a list of possible day-trade candidates by screening for the following criteria: price, average volume, and beta (a measure of stock volatility relative to the S&P500). More specifically, I recommend screening per the following settings:

- Price: > $20
- Average Volume: > 1million
- Beta: greater than 2.0 (2x more volatile than the S&P 500)

When day-trading, we want to work with only liquid, volatile, and higher priced stocks. We want stocks that move as far as possible, dollar-wise, in the least amount of time. A big mistake many beginning day-traders make is to trade the lower-priced stocks. You cannot make a sustained living day-trading low-priced stocks. The problem with lower-priced stocks is that as your account grows, and you take larger and larger positions, you will find it difficult to get in and out of the lower-priced stocks quickly. It is much easier to dump a 500 share position of a $100 stock without moving the bid-ask spread than a 5000 share position of a $10 stock.

Conversely, you can make a nice living simply day-trading a mere 100 shares of a stock like LNKD (LinkedIn, $250/share), 50 shares of CMG (Chipotle, $550) or even 10 shares of PCLN (Priceline, $1400/share). For example, if you average +0.20% net on a $250 stock on 5 daily trades, that's $250 net profit per day (less a mere $5 in commissions if you use Interactive Brokers).

On 250 annual trading days, that's a yearly income of more than $60,000...trading a single lot of 100 shares.

Now imagine you are trading 200 shares ($120,000!), 400 shares ($240,000), even 1000 shares ($600,000). Those are major league returns, and all scalable because you are not trading enough size to move the spread more than a few cents. But with lower priced stocks you would have to multiply these share counts 10 times or more to attain the same result. At these higher levels, your commissions costs increase and your fill prices suffer. When we are looking at net profits measured in the tenths of one percent, this makes a huge difference.

Note that it may be necessary, depending on market conditions, to fiddle a bit with the numbers of this simple watch list screen. In a breakaway bull market of the kind we saw in the late 1990's, we may need to raise our stock price range to capture the higher priced "big movers". In bear markets you may find that many of the best day-trading stocks are trading under $50 per share. But in a healthy bull market, which we prefer trading, most of the stocks we will be looking at trade at $50 per share or higher.

If the above screen returns, say, more than 100 candidates, then one can raise the average volume number to limit our selection to only the most liquid stocks. And lastly, when the market goes into a quiet period without much movement, we may not be able to find many stocks trading at a 2.0 beta. This figure may need to be lowered.

Once this screen returns a list of stocks (you should have more than 75; and if less, try lowering the beta figure), sort the list by order of decreasing beta and take the first 75 stocks. Then sort this list again by decreasing price, and take the top 50 of those stocks. These are the stocks you are going to monitor daily for DT setups. You don't want more than 50, because in certain market conditions you will register too many setups to trade. Nor do you want to limit your list to much less than 50, because in non-trending markets you may not have any setups at all.

Once you have your list of 50 stocks, write these into your charting software and save them as a watch list. Once you have inputted your watch list of stocks, you then will have the list or lists of stocks whose charts you will "eyeball" each trading day for possible day-trade setups. Note that those who are using Metastock or other real-time scanning software with intraday capability, and who have knowledge of trade scan programming language, can harness the power of a scanning tool to do at least some of the "eye-balling" for them. But even then, you will still need to take a good close look at each passing candidate's chart to make sure it fully satisfies the parameters of the trading system (as explained below). And in some cases, there are system parameters than cannot be scanned for, so in the end, there is really no way to avoid the more labor-intensive work of checking the charts one by one.

Your primary watch list will need to be updated once a week. In this way your watch list will rotate in and out of the most volatile, and hence most profitable, stocks. You will repeat the same process as listed above: screen for price, volume and beta; select the 50 highest beta stocks; and input these into your charting software as a watch list. You will find from week to week that the list does not change all that much. The same great trading vehicles keep showing up on the list. But you should be replacing about 5 to 10 of your stocks at each new screening.

Set Up Your Charting Workstation

Once you decide which charting service you are going to use, you will want to set up a number chart templates. These default templates are what you will use to find the trading setups in the DT systems taught below.

You will want to set up 5 chart templates as per the parameters listed below. You will also want to make sure that you have immediate access to a Time and Sales (T&S) window that links to each chart template, and a Market Watch quote box that includes the real-time quotes for Nasdaq, S&P500, the Dow, the Russell 2000, and the VIX Index (or the ETF equivalents for each).

Here are the system parameters what you want to put in your 5 chart templates (see key below):

- Chart 1:
  o Time: daily
  o Symbol: stock from watch list
  o Chart Type: candlesticks
  o Overlays: 20sma, 50sma, 200sma
  o Oscillators: Stochastics (5-3-1)

- Chart 2:
  o Time: hourly
  o Symbol: stock from watch list
  o Chart Type: candlesticks
  o Overlays: 20ma, 50ma, 200ma
  o Oscillators: MACD Histogram (12-26-9)

- Chart 3:
  - Time: 5min
  - Symbol: stock from watch list
  - Chart Type: candlesticks
  - Overlays: 20sma, 50sma, 200sma
  - Oscillators: Stochastics (5-3-1)

- Chart 4:
  - Time: 1min
  - Symbol: NQ (e-mini Nasdaq futures)
  - Chart Type: candlesticks
  - Overlays: 20sma, 50sma
  - Oscillators: none

- Chart 5:
  - Time: 1min
  - Symbol: ES (e-mini S&P100 futures)
  - Chart Type: candlesticks
  - Overlays: 20sma, 50sma
  - Oscillators: none

On all 5 charts you want to put a lock on the "interval" button so that the time frame remains the same in each for every stock you look at. Charts 1 – 3 are going to be used to look at charts of the stocks on the watch list you created as per the instructions listed above. In these charts, therefore, you want to keep the "symbol" button open so that you can apply the template to each of the stocks on your watch list. If you have done this properly, then every time you click on a new stock in your watch list, that stock should appear in all 3 chart windows at daily, hourly and 5min. intervals respectively. If you are not sure how to do this in your particular charting package, you'll need to check the Help sections of your service. Note that this kind of multiple chart view can only be done in TradingView with a premium subscription.

To give you an idea of what your chart template should look like, I include here below a picture of SPX500 (the S&P 500 Index) on chart template 1 as described above. You'll note the 3 moving averages overlaid on the candlestick chart, and the Stochastics (5-3-3) below the chart. The oversold and overbought lines are inputted by default at 20 and 80 respectively. You can adjust these as needed.

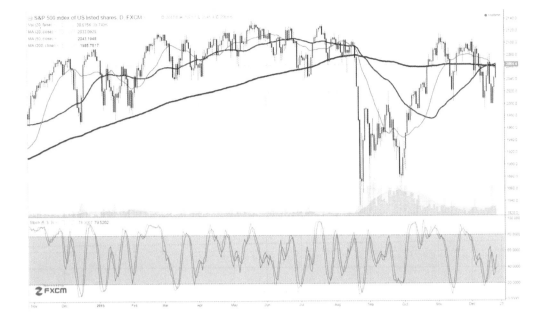

Chart templates 4 and 5 will be used to keep track of the minute by minute movements of the primary index futures. On these charts, therefore, you will want to lock in the symbol as well as the time interval.

You want the time and sales window to show the order flow for each stock you are looking at from your watch list, so be sure that the "symbol" button is on open on the T&S window. There is no interval button for Time and Sales.

Once all this is done, and after you have inputted the 50 or so stocks from your scan into a watch list, then save the workstation. This should now be the station that opens up every time you start your charting service, and it is the primary source of information you will use to enter and exit your day-trades.

Note: with 8 data windows open inside your charting workstation, it is imperative that you have as much desktop space as possible. For this reason you should consider buying the largest monitor you can afford, or even consider using a double- or triple-screen monitor (see our "Hardware" section above).

Becoming a Tape Reader

There are two skills that a trader must possess in order to become proficient at DT: sound chart reading and sound tape reading. The first we will describe below as we lay out the parameters of the trading systems, while the second is outlined here.

Tape reading gets its name from the old "ticker tape" machine that used to feed stock quotes to brokers before the advent of computers and LED displays. A small, glass enclosed printing press would spit out a tape listing quotes throughout the day as trades were executed. Fortunately, we no longer have to wait patiently for the tape to give us a quote on the stock we are interested in. We simply type the symbol into our Qcharts and we are given a trade by trade "tape" of the action in real-time.

Here is what the old "ticker tape" machine looked like:

If you read through the great stories in Jack Schwaeger's 4-volume series, *Market Wizards*, you will find a common theme running throughout the various biographies collected there: tape reading. Besides having nerves of steel, most of the world's greatest traders are also great tape readers. Many began their careers trading "nothing but the tape".

Floor traders live and die by the tape. They don't have the luxury of sitting quietly in front of a computer all day analyzing charts. They can only trade the ebb and flow of orders as they occur throughout the day. It is a bit of a "chicken and egg" phenomenon, here, because floor traders with their frequent quick-turn trading techniques create the very tape they are trading. But other than rumors that filter past their trading stations, they have nothing else to go on but the tape.

Some of the tape reading skill is simply a product of intuition. If you are a strong intuitive type, you already have a head start on developing this skill. Those able to hear a piece of music, and anticipate what the next movement will be before it comes; or those who in listening to someone talk will finish his or her sentences; are those who are strong intuitive types and will likely make great tape

readers.

But there is also a science to tape reading which can be taught, and fortunately it is not "rocket science"! Moreover, there is a discipline I will teach you here as well that can sharpen what little intuitive power you may possess into a tremendous, profit-making talent.

First, let's talk about the science. For the purposes of DT, there are 3 primary sources of the "tape" as we now know it: Time and Sales (T&S), the bid x ask sizing that you see in your online brokers trading workstation (where you place your trades), and Level II quotes. For the purposes of this manual, I will not be talking about Level II. Using this tool is more art than science, and in any case, algo

Let's start with the first, T&S.

Your **T&S indicator** should look something like this (stock: CSIQ):

Time	BATE	Size	Price	Exch	Indicator
15:13:38	Ask	100	28.4300	cinc	
15:13:38	Bid	1,200	28.3800	cinc	
15:13:38	Ask	100	28.4200	cinc	
15:13:37	Trade	400	28.4200	cinc	
15:13:37	Trade	3,700	28.4200	cinc	
15:13:37	Trade	100	28.4200	cinc	
15:13:37	Best ask	3,000	28.4200	nasd	
15:13:37	Ask	200	28.4200	cinc	
15:13:37	Ask	5,300	28.4200	cinc	
15:13:37	Bid	100	28.3800	cinc	
15:13:36	Trade	500	28.3800	pacx	
15:13:36	Best bid	1,100	28.3800	nasd	
15:13:36	Bid	800	28.3800	pacx	
15:13:36	Ask	5,100	28.4200	cinc	
15:13:36	Bid	100	28.3800	cinc	
15:13:36	Ask	5,300	28.4200	cinc	
15:13:36	Bid	100	28.3800	cinc	
15:13:35	Ask	1,500	28.4100	pacx	
15:13:35	Best ask	3,000	28.4200	nasd	
15:13:35	Ask	100	28.4700	amex	
15:13:35	Ask	100	28.4600	amex	
15:13:34	Trade	300	28.4200	cinc	
15:13:34	Trade	300	28.4200	cinc	
15:13:34	Trade	100	28.4200	cinc	
15:13:34	Trade	300	28.4200	bost	

In the T&S above we see the order flow of CSIQ trading near the close on 12/21/2015. I have adjusted the default color settings to fit my tape reading needs. The color coding I use is as follows:

- light green = buys at the ask
- red = sells at the bid
- white = trades between bid and ask (not seen here)
- yellow = new bids ("best bid" = inside bid)

- gray = new asks ("best ask" = inside ask)
- blue = new high of the day (not seen here)
- orange = new low of the day (not seen here)

[NOTE: those of you reading a hard copy of this manual may not be able to see these colors in the image above.]

The T&S marks order flow in a given stock. When you are tape reading from T&S, you are looking at 3 distinct kinds of changes in order flow:

- *color changes*
- *position size changes*
- *rate of trade changes*

Color changes. This is what we learn from these color changes. During a bullish turn in the market, we will see lots of yellow and green. During a bearish turn, we will see lots of gray and red. A steady flow of new bids and buys at the ask indicates that buyers are in charge of the market and that the price of the stock is rising and should continue to rise over the near-term. A steady flow of new asks and sells at the bid indicates that sellers are in charge of the market and that the price of the stock is falling and should continue to fall over the near-term. If the market is neutral (no one color dominates) and then suddenly you see a new flow of yellow and green, you know that the price has built a short-term base and that buyers are now stepping up, causing price to likely begin rising in the short term. If the market is neutral and then suddenly you see a flow of gray and red, you know that the price has built a short-term base and that sellers are now stepping up, causing price to likely begin falling in the short term. So to summarize:

- steady flow of yellow and green = price to continue to rise
- steady flow of gray and red = price to continue to fall
- change from neutral to yellow and green = price about to rise
- change from neutral to gray and red = price about to fall

In the CSIQ T&S above, the market is currently neutral. Bulls and bears are in a tug-of-war and are battling it out for domination. While there is more buying (green) than selling (red), the size on the ask (sellers) is larger than that seen on the bid (buyers).

Size changes. Here we are looking at the size of the orders coming in at the bid and ask, and the size of the orders being executed. Color changes are only as good as the size behind them. Seeing lots of yellow and green is great if you are long, but it is even better if the numbers going with them are high. In the URBN example below, we see a market in bullish mode. We see lots of green buying with large orders going through, and big bets being made at the bid. By

contrast, the bets made at the offer or ask are much smaller. And indeed, the 5 min chart on this day (11/25/2015) shows URBN in the middle of a nice $0.90 (3.8%) ramp up:

Time	BATE	Size	Price	Exch	Indicator
15:56:44	Best ask	48,500	23.8100	nasd	
15:56:44	Ask	100	23.8200	nasd	
15:56:43	Trade	300	23.8100	cinc	
15:56:43	Trade	2,200	23.8100	cinc	
15:56:42	Trade	1,000	23.8100	cinc	
15:56:42	Trade	1,500	23.8100	cinc	
15:56:42	Trade	2,000	23.8100	cinc	
15:56:42	Trade	700	23.8100	pacx	
15:56:42	Trade	100	23.8100	cinc	
15:56:42	Ask	300	23.8100	cinc	
15:56:42	Bid	46,900	23.8100	pacx	
15:56:42	Best bid	67,200	23.8000	nasd	
15:56:42	Bid	41,900	23.8100	pacx	
15:56:42	Ask	4,700	23.8100	pacx	
15:56:42	Bid	100	23.8000	pacx	
15:56:42	Ask	5,400	23.8100	pacx	
15:56:42	Ask	1,600	23.8100	cinc	
15:56:42	Ask	5,400	23.8100	pacx	
15:56:42	Best bid	67,200	23.8000	nasd	
15:56:41	Ask	6,900	23.8100	pacx	
15:56:40	Ask	12,400	23.8100	cinc	
15:56:40	Bid	100	23.8000	cinc	
15:56:40	Trade	300	23.8100	pacx	
15:56:39	Ask	5,600	23.8100	pacx	
15:56:38	Best bid	65,700	23.8000	nasd	

Here is what the chart of URBN looked like while this T&S reading above was taken.

Now look at what the URBN chart looked like a little while later as day-traders began taking profits off the table and sellers ruled the tape.

If we look at what was going on in the T&S window shortly after the rally in URBN shares began to top out, we will see a tape that was turning decidedly bearish. We see not only bearish changes in the color of the tape, we also see bearish changes in size as larger orders start coming in on the ask:

Time	BATE	Size	Price	Exch	Indicator
15:58:56	Ask	50,400	23.8200	cinc	
15:58:56	Best bid	10,800	23.8100	nasd	
15:58:56	Bid	10,000	23.8100	cinc	
15:58:55	Best ask	35,500	23.8200	nasd	
15:58:55	Bid	6,900	23.8100	pacx	
15:58:55	Best ask	32,500	23.8200	nasd	
15:58:55	Best bid	10,800	23.8100	nasd	
15:58:55	Trade	850	23.8100	bost	
15:58:55	Trade	900	23.8100	bost	
15:58:55	Trade	1,500	23.8100	bost	
15:58:55	Trade	895	23.8100	bost	
15:58:55	Ask	16,700	23.8100	pacx	
15:58:55	Bid	7,200	23.8100	pacx	
15:58:55	Bid	7,500	23.8100	pacx	
15:58:55	Best bid	7,000	23.8100	nasd	
15:58:55	Best ask	27,300	23.8200	nasd	
15:58:55	Trade	355	23.8100	bost	
15:58:55	Best bid	7,700	23.8100	nasd	
15:58:55	Best ask	25,100	23.8200	nasd	
15:58:55	Bid	6,000	23.8100	pacx	
15:58:55	Trade	300	23.8100	cinc	
15:58:55	Trade	100	23.8100	cinc	
15:58:55	Trade	200	23.8100	cinc	
15:58:55	Trade	2,000	23.8100	cinc	
15:58:55	Trade	200	23.8100	cinc	

Speed changes. The last element of information that Time and Sales conveys to the trader is the speed at which the "tape" scrolls past your screen. In quiet periods, the tape will move slowly with only a few new ticks every minute or so. But at reversal periods, when new traders are jumping on board (or making a quick exit), the speed of the scrolling can increase dramatically.

Of course, the speed of the T&S tape is relative to how actively the stock is traded on any given day. In a heavily traded security (e.g., MSFT, AAPL, SPY, QQQ, etc.), the scrolling speed can change from fast to *very* fast. But in less active securities, the T&S can sit quietly for minutes at a time, barely moving, until a new wave of buying or selling takes over. It is important to note, therefore, that it is the change in movement that is the key to confirming the new or continuing trend, not the actual speed of the tape.

So let me summarize our T&S "tape reading" rules. Putting it all together, here is what you will be looking for. I like to use "green light" and "red light" as signals for timely buys and sells:

- predominance of yellow and green = green light
- predominance of gray and red = red light

- size on yellow and green = green light
- size on gray and red = red light

- speeding up of scrolling = green light
- slowing down of scrolling = red light

- to enter a new long (or cover a short) = 3 green lights
- to enter a new short (or sell a long) = 2 red lights and 1 green light.

Of course, we don't always get our ideal timing scenario, and other factors may force us to enter the trade regardless of the tape. And to be sure, you can learn profitable day-trading without using the Time & Sales indicator. But with a tape reading skill in your trading arsenal, you have an objective strategy that will help you more precisely time your entries and exits. Given that in DT it is often a matter of mere pennies that separate a profitable trade from an unprofitable one, the tape reading skill is certainly one to consider working on.

The other tool we use to "read the tape" is the simple **bid x ask** and **last size** quotes that you'll find in your trading workstation. Of course, Time & Sales gives you this same information, but with everything else you are looking at there, it is best to use your workstation for this information.

Here is what you will likely see for a given stock in your trading workstation. I'll use ORCL as an example:

ORCL	45	11.17	11.18	116	11.17	20

The numbers following the stock symbol, from left to right, are as follows: size on the bid, current inside bid, current inside ask, size on the ask, last price traded, last size traded.

Here is what these numbers mean:

- the *size on the bid* (45) indicates the number of shares (x 100) that are currently being bid for the stock, i.e., buyers seeking sellers

- the *inside bid* (11.17) is the best price at which one can currently sell the stock

- the *inside ask* (11.18) is the best price at which one can currently buy the stock

- the *size on the ask* (116) indicates the number of shares (x 100) that are currently on offer for the stock, i.e., sellers seeking buyers

- the *last price traded* indicates the price at which shares of the stock last changed hands (11.17)

- and the *last size traded* indicates the number of shares that were traded at that price

Now, just from these numbers alone I can tell a lot about what "mood" the stock is currently in. I know, for example, that would-be sellers outnumber would-be buyers by almost 3 to 1. And I know that the last trade executed was a sale of 2000 shares at the bid, which confirms my bearish suspicions.

Watching these numbers change over time can give us even more information. In general the rules are simple:

- as ask size increases and more trades of large size go off at the bid, there is selling pressure and the stock is likely to go down over the next few minutes;

- as bid size increases and more trades of large size go off at the ask, there is buying pressure and the stock is likely to go up over the next few minutes.

So, if you want to short but see buying pressure: you wait it out. And if you want to go long but see selling pressure: you wait it out. When the tide turns (and it always does), you jump on board and enjoy the near-term ride.

Here is an example of increasing sell pressure in ORCL:

ORCL	45	11.17	11.18	116	11.17	20
ORCL	25	11.17	11.18	132	11.18	8
ORCL	12	11.17	11.18	154	11.17	32
ORCL	10	11.17	11.18	155	11.18	1
ORCL	7	11.17	11.18	185	11.17	5
ORCL	1	11.17	11.18	238	11.17	23

In this example, we can be reasonably sure that the 11.17 bid is about to drop to the next lower level (likely 11.16) and that the offer will also drop down in a chase to reach equilibrium. Here is an example of the opposite, increasing buying pressure:

ORCL	45	11.17	11.18	116	11.17	20
ORCL	85	11.17	11.18	97	11.18	32
ORCL	105	11.17	11.18	75	11.18	5

| ORCL | 185 | 11.17 | 11.18 | 55 | 11.18 | 25 |
| ORCL | 208 | 11.17 | 11.18 | 23 | 11.17 | 3 |

We can safely assume here that that offer at 11.18 will not last long. One more sizeable buy should cause the tape to move up to the next level (11.18 x 11.19). If we are looking to establish a long position in ORCL, we will want to jump on 11.18 before it disappears. If we are looking to short ORCL, then we will stand aside until we see selling pressure begin to develop.

It needs to be said that turns of the tape do not last long. The kind of information tape watching provides is normally for the very short term. But what can convey a larger picture is a "tape reading pattern", where you see either buying or selling pressure develop repeatedly over a given period of time and/or repeatedly at a given price level. This would indicate a trend that can be traded.

There are other patterns that tape reading can signal. For example, repeated failures to take down a large number of shares at a given offer can convey a pattern we would recognize as "resistance". Likewise, repeated failures to erase a large number of shares at a given bid can convey a pattern we would recognize as "support". And consequently, we can predict a breakout or breakdown as that offer or bid is hammered at repeatedly until it finally gives way. Jumping on board just as the last shares are taken out is one of the most thrilling parts of trading the tape!

How to Train your Tape Reading Intuition

I have now described the "science" part of tape reading. But let's put that together with an emphasis on developing your tape reading "intuition". To do that, I want to suggest an exercise you can do as you are watching the tape during the trading day:

- pick an actively traded, volatile stock (any of the stocks on your watch list as per the scan above will suit this exercise), preferably one that typically maintains a bid-ask spread of 0.01

- watch both T&S and the bid x ask change over a period of about an hour

- do not glance at any chart; watch only the tape

- with a notepad nearby, mark the price at which you think a change in direction is coming

- then mark again the price when you think that direction has stalled or is about to reverse

- do this twice per day between 9:30 and 10:30 am, EST, and 15:00 to 16:00, EST (the most active trading hours)

- use the same stock at all times

- keep track of your profits and losses in each hour session

- do this every day for 10 trading days

By the end of this exercise (2 weeks later) you should be a proficient tape reader. You will develop a feel for points of support and resistance in your stock. You will catch the breakouts and breakdowns. You will scalp the whips and ride the waves. You should also know whether you tend to be a better morning or afternoon trader. And believe me, your overall trading will improve dramatically...just by reading the tape alone!

4. FIVE DAY-TRADING SYSTEMS

We come now to the "meat" of this manual: how and when to enter and exit day-trades for maximum profits with minimal risk. If you have skipped down to this section first without reading the foregoing, please go back! You will need to read the preceding sections in order to understand fully what is going to be said from here on.

Ok, so you are ready to begin the great and profitable adventure of day-trading. Let's assume that you are going the full trading day from open to close. It should be noted that not all of the following DT systems are able to be traded all day. The first two systems are only able to be traded in the morning after the open, and the latter six systems are only able to be traded after the first hour of trading has passed. But we will assume here that you are one of the lucky ones who has the full day to devote to cranking up the ole' day-trading ATM-machine.

Know Your Candlesticks

Before we look at any DT systems we need to say a word about candlestick formations. Candlestick formations play an important role in selecting appropriate stocks for DT. While High Frequency Trading (HFT) and mechanical, algorithmic trading have worked to make candlestick formations less reliable in recent years, they nevertheless continue to serve our DT purposes. If you are not familiar with some of the more basic candlestick formations, and with such terms as "tails" or "shadows", "dojis", "hammers" and "stars", then you need to take a candlestick primer.

Fortunately there are several such courses available on the internet for free. Perhaps the best of these is offered by Stockcharts.com and can be accessed here: http://stockcharts.com/education/ChartAnalysis/candlesticks.html

The key components to a candlestick are as follows:

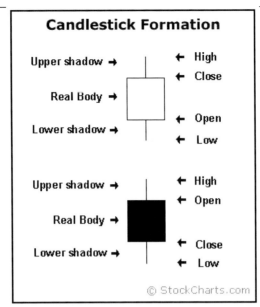

We want to pay attention especially to what the above chart calls "shadows" (upper and lower) – I call them "tails" – and to the color of the "real body." Here the real body is colored either black or white. In most charting packages, the real body will be colored red or green. A white or green real body is generally indicative of a bullish trading period (the length of which is determined by what chart periodicity you are looking at), while a black or red real body can indicate a bearish period. This is particularly true when you see a number of white/green candles in a row, or their opposite.

Take a look at this chart comparison for the Nasdaq 100 ETF (the symbol is now QQQ). You can see how mutli-day swings higher are dominated by white candles, while swings lower are dominated by black candles. You can also see the advantage a candlestick chart has over a simple bar chart. The former gives us much more information than the latter, and it makes it stand out in clearly visible form:

So again, if you are not familiar with the basic of candlestick charting, please do not proceed until you have taken a good look at the Stockcharts.com candlestick primer linked above.

With that said, it is time now to move on to our first DT trading system.

System #1: The Bullish Counter-trend Gap Down System

This bullish setup, along with its bearish compliment, the "Counter-trend Gap Up", is one of the most profitable setups available to the day-trader. It is also one of the easiest to trade, since it requires no indicators, no moving averages, and no references to volume or Time & Sales. While you can use your tape reading skills to make your entry more precise, they are not needed to trade this system profitably.

There is, however, one problem with both the Counter-trend systems as outlined here: when it fails, it tends to fail spectacularly. So if you plan on trading this setup, you must use a stop-loss to protect yourself against large losses, and be disciplined with its application.

As you scan your 50-stock watch list right at the open, here is what you are looking for:

1) A stock in a modest to strong uptrend...defined as:
   a) The 50sma is above the 200sma on the DAILY chart
   b) And both ma's, preferably, are upsloping

2) Which has gapped down at the open...defined as:
   a) an opening trade BELOW the intraday LOW of the previous day

3) And which after 10 minutes of trading is showing signs of bullish trading activity...to be defined below.

Once you have a short list of stocks from your watch list that satisfy the first two criteria, here is how you will find stocks that satisfy the third criteria, and then how to trade them for profit:

- **Entry signal:** in this system we define "bullish trading activity" (criterion 3 above) as a break above the high of the first 10-minutes of trading, preferably coupled with significant "tape" strength (though this is not strictly required)

- **Entry order:** buy only on a stop-market order set 2 cents above the 10-minute high of the day; alternatively, you can enter once the 10-minute high is broken AND you see bullish tape activity using tape reading skills as outline above

- **Stop-loss:** as long as you are trading one of the stocks from your watch list (which are higher priced, very liquid, and sufficiently volatile), you can use a -1.25% to -1.5% stop-loss price; at 2.0% profit move stop to breakeven

- **_Adjusting Stop-loss:_** if the trade moves to a 1% profit, move your stop-loss to a -0.75% level; if the trade moves to a 2% profit, move the stop-loss to breakeven (i.e., $0.01 above your entry to cover commissions)

- **_Exit:_** on a trigger of the stop-loss, on significant "tape" weakness (optional), or on market close, whichever comes first

Often a decent company will experience a gap down during a bullish trending period (as measured by the 50sma over the 200sma) because they missed earnings expectations, or were downgraded, or made an unexpected share offering to raise cash. Quite often these are buying opportunities for the alert day-trader.

Such was the case for TRIP after it reported a big earnings miss. It took a couple hours for traders to erase the supply of shares, but once they did, it was all uphill, netting a nice $1.40 gain per share for a 4-hour trade:

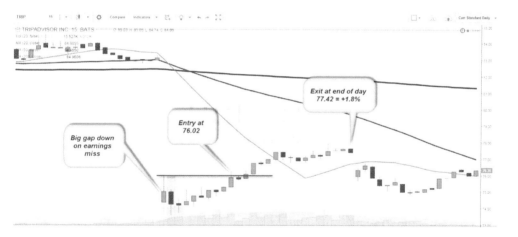

REMEMBER: as tempting as it may be to jump on the opening gap right away, do not enter until the 10minute high of the day has been taken out. These trades can fail spectacularly, and one way to minimize this is to make sure we are trading up into new high territory after the "morning noise" has dissipated.

System #2: The Bearish Countertrend Gap Up System

This bearish setup is the counterpart of the bullish "Countertrend Gap Down" formation. Like that setup, it is one of the easiest to trade, since it requires no indicators, no moving averages, and no references to volume or trade rate. But again: when it fails, it tends to fail in a big way. So if you plan on trading this setup, you must use a stop-loss and be disciplined with its application.

As you scan your 50-stock watch list right at the open, here is what you are looking for:

1) A stock in a modest to strong downtrend...defined as:
  a) The 50sma is below the 200sma on the DAILY chart
  b) And both ma's, preferably, are down-sloping

2) Which has gapped up at the open...defined as:
  a) an opening trade ABOVE the intraday HIGH of the previous day

3) And which after 10 minutes of trading is showing signs of bearish trading activity...to be defined below.

Once you have a short list of stocks from your watch list that satisfy the first two criteria, here is how you will find stocks that satisfy the third criteria, and then how to trade them for profit:

- **Entry signal:** in this system we define "bearish trading activity" (criterion 3 above) as a break below the low of the first 10-minutes of trading, preferably coupled with significant "tape" weakness (though this is not strictly required)

- **Entry order:** sell short only on a stop-market order set 2 cents below the 10-minute low of the day; alternatively, you can enter once the 10-minute low is broken AND you see bearish tape activity using tape reading skills as outline above

- **Stop-loss:** as long as you are trading one of the stocks from your watch list (which are higher priced, very liquid, and sufficiently volatile), you can use a +1.25% to +1.5% stop-loss price; at 2.0% profit move stop to breakeven

- **Adjusting Stop-loss:** if the trade moves to a 1% profit, move your stop-loss to a -0.75% level; if the trade moves to a 2% profit, move the stop-loss to breakeven (i.e., $0.01 above your entry to cover commissions)

- **Exit:** on a trigger of the stop-loss, on significant "tape" weakness (optional), or on market close, whichever comes first

Here is a classic example of a Countertrend Gap Up play. XPO had been in a steep selloff for several months. On 12/17/15, the stock gapped up at the open, but then quickly started to selloff. At 9:40 am, EST, we put a sell short stop order at 28.62, and once it filled (3 minutes later) we set a stop loss order at 29.05. Later that morning we were able to move our stop to breakeven. Fortunately the stock never came close to stopping out. Instead it continued to fall into the close, netting us a nice 1-day profit of 6.9% (about $200 for each 100 shares).

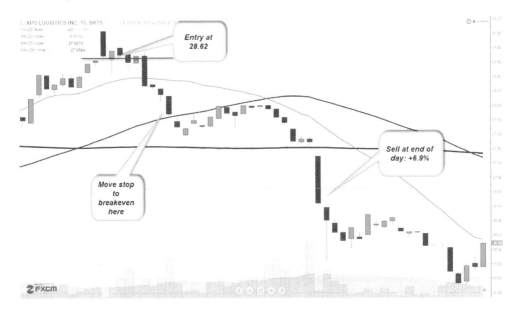

REMEMBER: do not enter until the 10minute low of the day has been taken out. These trades can fail spectacularly, and one way to minimize this is to make sure we are trading down into new low territory after the "morning noise" has dissipated.

System #3: The Bullish MA-Tag

Before we begin to look for Bullish MA-Tags, we want to make sure we have the general market's order flow on our side. This means that we want to enter Bullish MA-Tags only when the general market itself is in a bullish mood. The best way to tell what mood the market is in is to check the E-mini futures.

To do this we will use the E-mini futures to set up what I call a "Market Mood Box" (MMB). For this we will use an intraday chart of ES, the e-Mini futures contract for the S&P500. Here is the technique for setting up the MMB:

1) Wait until 10:30 am, EST (i.e., after 1 hour of trading)
2) Place a horizontal line over the intraday high of ES
3) Place a 2nd horizontal line under the intraday low of ES
4) Place a 3rd horizontal line at the midpoint between these two lines
5) These three lines form the MMB
6) The MMB gives us either a "green" or "red" light for trading the Bullish MA-tag system
    i) We use the system when ES is trading in the upper half of or above the MMB
    ii) We do not use the system when ES is trading in the lower half or below the MMB

For this system we will be trading from a 5-minute chart loaded with the following indicators:

- *Candlesticks*
- *50sma and 200sma*
- *Slow Stochastics set at 5-3-3*

So let's assume now that we have a green light from the MMB to use the Bullish MA-tag system. We then scan our watch list for stocks making the following formation:

1) **The stock is in an uptrend on the DAILY chart** (for this system we want the daily 50ma above the daily 200ma, with current price above the 200sma, and both sma's preferably are upsloping)

2) **On the 5min. chart, price has rallied up into either the 50ma or the 200ma and some part of the candle has touched that MA line (the "tag")**

3) **The %K Stochastics Line (5-3-3) is currently under 25**

(under 20 even better)

4) A green candle has formed with a closing price in the upper 1/3rd of the candle and above the MA tagged

- ○ **Entry signal:** enter on first trade above the high of the green signal candle coupled with significant "tape" strength

- ○ **Stop:** use -1.5% stop; set at breakeven once trade moves to +2% profit

- ○ **Exit:** on stop, on significant "tape" weakness", or on market close

With the Bullish MA-tag, it is possible to get more than one trade per day from a given stock. In the following chart of TNA (3x Bull Smallcap Index), we see 2 profitable Bullish MA-tag trades yielding a total gain of +2.3%. Here is how they break down:

After determining that the MMB has given a green light for the Bullish MA-tag system, we looking for chart in a daily uptrend with a pullback on the 5-min. chart to either the 50 or the 200sma. We see that at point A. This was coupled with a Stochastics (5-3-3) reading below 20 (ideal) and a green candle. We then went long on the first tick above the high of that green candle, marked by point C. At point D we exited the trade on significant tape weakness. We then re-entered on a new signal (E/F/G) and sold at the close. Together these two trades netted us a nice $155 per 100 shares traded.

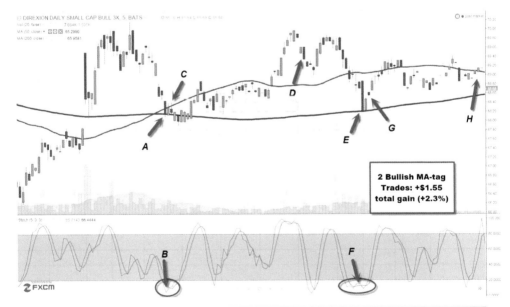

System #4: The Bearish MA-Tag

The Bearish MA-Tag is simply the inverse of the Bullish MA-Tag. Again, before we look for Bearish MA-Tags, we want to make sure we have the general market's order flow on our side. This means that we want to enter Bearish MA-Tags only when the general market itself is in a bearish mood. We will again use the MMB as above, only now we get a "green" light to use the Bearish MA-tag system when the ES is trading in the lower half or below the MMB. Once we get this green light, we will use the Bearish MA-tag to find profitable trades on the short side of the market.

Ok, let's assume now that we have a green light from the MMB to go short using the Bearish MA-tag system. So we then scan our watch list for stocks making the following formation:

1) **The stock is in an downtrend on the DAILY chart** (for this system we want the daily 50ma below the daily 200ma, with current price below the 200sma, and both sma's preferably are down-sloping)

2) **On the 5min. chart, price has pulled back into either the 50ma or the 200ma and some part of the candle has touched that MA line (the "tag")**

3) **The %K Stochastics Line (5-3-3) is currently over 75 (over 80 even better)**

4) **A red candle has formed with a closing price in the lower 1/3rd of the candle and below the MA tagged**

○ **Entry signal:** enter on first trade below the low of the red signal candle coupled with significant "tape" strength

○ **Stop:** use -1.5% stop; set at breakeven once trade moves to +2% profit

○ **Exit:** on stop, on significant "tape" weakness", or on market close

In the chart below you will see two profitable Bearish MA-tag trades completed on two consecutive days. These were in the stock, CAR, which at the time was the stock on my list with the highest beta value.

In the first trade, you will see the setup at A with a tag of the 50sma, a red candle, and a trade below that candle's low, coupled with a Stochastics reading above 80. This trade was held into the close (C) for a nice gain of +4.9%.

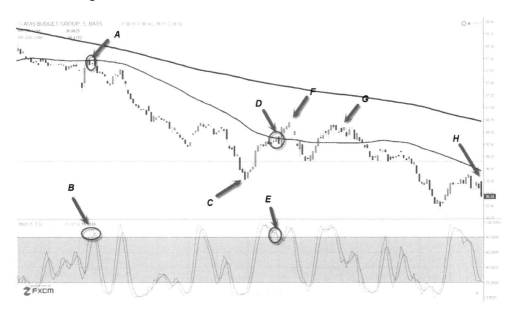

In the second trade at D, coupled with a high Stochastics reading at E, initially went the wrong direction. The highs of F and G, however, did not penetrate our stop-loss, so we stayed with the trade through these "head-fake" moves. Again, the trade was held to the close for another gain of +2.3%. An investment of $10,000 would have yielded a two-day gain of $720 from this stock. Nice!

System #5: The Long-Short Mac-Stoch System

I'm going to introduce you to one of my favorite setups here. It also happens to be a great swing trade setup as well. When combined with tape reading skills it makes for a very profitable DT approach. Overall, this DT system has proven to be my most profitable. You can make a very good living trading this one system alone. It takes a bit more work than the previously described systems, but once you get the hang of it you'll see just how easy it is to trade.

I am presenting this system as a combined system, with both a long and short variation, rather than treat them as separate systems. I like to trade this system in its two iterations concurrently. In other words, I use the Mac-Stoch system to find both long and short trades on the same day (in different stocks, of course). Typically when I trade the Mac-Stoch system, I might have up to ten trades on at the same time, some of which are long and some of which are short. While that may sound like a lot of confusion, you'll see that you might have 10 trades on at once but in only two different stocks. This is system that will identify multiple trades per day in the same stock. We will thus be using a "scaling in" technique (described below) to manage our trades.

The Mac-Stoch system uses 2 charts simultaneously: an hourly chart which will tell you whether to go long or short, and a 5 min. chart which will tell you when to enter and exit the trade. If you want to use this as a swing trade setup, the 2 charts you would use are the weekly and daily charts. In this manual I will focus only on the DT version of the system.

On the hourly chart, you want the MACD Histogram as your only indicator. You'll want the Histogram set at 12-26-9, which is the default setting for most charting packages. The MACD Histogram, which is a function of the MACD itself, is a lagging momentum indicator and gives very simple readings of the current trend (in this case, the hourly trend). A MACD Histogram reading above the 0-line indicates a bullish trend, while a Histogram reading below the 0-line indicates a bearish trend. For clarity, I like to set the color of my Histogram to show green when bullish, and red when bearish. Needless to say, when we get a bullish MACD Histogram reading on the hourly chart, we will only look for a long signal, while a bearish Histogram reading forces us to look only for a short signal.

On the 5-min. chart, you will want only the Slow Stochastics (5-3-3) indicator. This indicator gives a potential buy signal when the %K line drops below to or below the 20 line, then crosses up over the slower

moving %D line. When we are looking for trades on the short side, the 5-minute Stochastics gives a potential short signal when %K rises to or above the 80 line, then crosses down over the slower moving %D line.

Note that these signals are only the initial signal of two signals needed to complete the setup. Before we enter the trade, we need to see a green candle that closes in the upper $1/3^{rd}$ of its candle (for longs) following the Stochastics cross, or the first red candle that closes in the lower $1/3^{rd}$ of its candle (for shorts).

So to summarize the Mac-Stoch system, this is what you will be looking for on the charts from your primary watch list (scrolling through one by one):

According to the Mach-Stoch system, you have a potentially valid LONG setup when...

> **1) MACD histogram on the hourly chart is green (above the 0-line)**
>
> **2) and %K Stochastics on the 5min chart goes to or below 20**
>
> **3) and then %K on 5min chart crosses above %D**

Alternatively, you have a potentially valid SHORT setup when...

> **1) MACD Histogram on the hourly chart is red (below the 0-line)**
>
> **2) and %K Stochastics on the 5min chart goes to or above 80**
>
> **3) and then %K on 5min chart crosses below %D**

Once you have a valid potential setup, here is how you manage the trade:

- ○ **Entry Signal for Longs:** after the above LONG setup criteria have been met, enter on the close of the first green candle that closes in the upper $1/3^{rd}$ of its candlestick

- ○ **Entry Signal for Shorts:** after the above SHORT setup criteria have been met, enter on the close of the first red candle that closes in the lower $1/3^{rd}$ of its candlestick

- o **Stop for Longs:** use -1.5% stop; move to breakeven at +2% profit

- o **Stop for Shorts:** use +1.5% stop; move to breakeven at +2% profit

- o **Exit for Longs:** on stop, on significant "tape" weakness, or on market close

- o **Exit for Shorts:** on stop, on significant "tape" strength, or on market close

In the chart below you will see the hourly chart of CAR (Avis Budget Group). I have highlighted a period in early October, 2015, where the MACD Histogram was registering an uptrend by keeping above the 0-line for several days. As you can see from the price chart, this Histogram signal coincided with a bullish move in the stock itself.

Now, once we step down to the 5-minute chart of CAR – the chart we will be taking our trades from (see below) – we can see that the period highlighted above on the hourly chart produced 10 long trades on the 5-minute chart. Remember, since the MACD on the hourly chart is green, we will only be going long. Of those 10 trades, 9 were winners. Even though several traded against us for a time, none reached our 1.5% stop-loss. In each case we held the trade to the close.

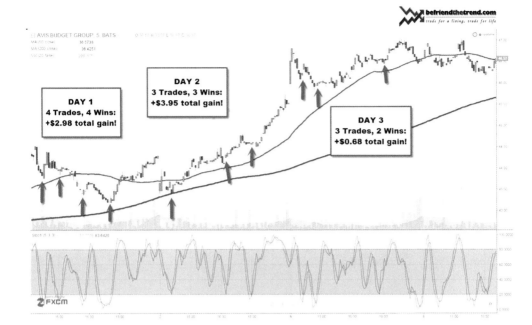

DAY 1
4 Trades, 4 Wins:
+$2.98 total gain!

DAY 2
3 Trades, 3 Wins:
+$3.95 total gain!

DAY 3
3 Trades, 2 Wins:
+$0.68 total gain!

Of course, the only way to capture all these gains is to take on multiple DT positions in the same stock. Since the Mac-Stoch system tends to trigger multiple trades per day per stock, it is best to use a "*scaling in*" approach by buying each entry signal in increments. It's rare to get more than 5 trade signals per day per stock using the Mac-Stoch system, so the best way to maximize your returns is to divide your trading capital into 5 equal lots, putting the same lot-size into the stock at each new signal, each with its own stop-loss based on your entry price. While the above 3-days of trading the Mac-Stoch system for CAR netted an outstanding $7.61 profit on 10 separate entries (only 3 exits, of course), or about 17% return, your true return on investment (ROI) is more like 3.4% (17% divided by 5). For only 3 days of trading, that is a phenomenal return.

Now let's look at the short side of the Mac-Stoch system. In the chart below of XIV (Inverse VIX Index), you will see a highlighted period showing a bearish MACD reading on the hourly chart. This gives us the "red" light we need to look for short setups from the system.

As we scroll down to the 5-minute chart for XIV for that same period, we will see 4 Mac-Stoch sell signals in play over two days. None of the trades hit the stop-loss so we held into the close. Our total net gain o the 4 entries (2 exits) was a whopping $8.18 (XIV is a great DT instrument!).

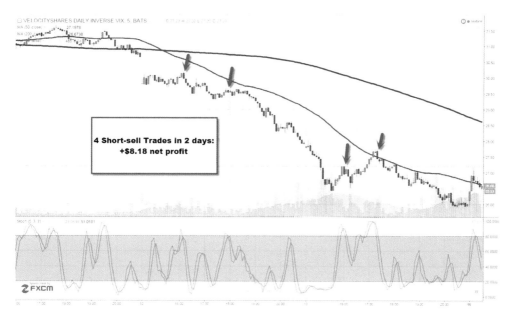

As per the example above, we would have scaled into these trades with only a portion of our allotted capital put into each entry signal.

While the $8.18 gain represents a gain of nearly +29% on the average entry price, our true net ROI would be more like +5.7% for two days of trading. Not bad at all!

There are two additional things to add regarding the trading protocol of the Mac-Stoch system. It is helpful if you can set up both the hourly and 5-minute chart in your charting package in such a way that both can be seen simultaneously. You will want to check the Histogram on an hourly basis to make sure that it remains in the direction of your trading. It is not uncommon to see a Histogram change from bullish to bearish, and vice versa, in the same trading day.

Also you might want to note that, as a general rule with this system, when the MACD Histogram spikes up or down with long bars relative to the length of nearby bars, it indicates that the trend is strong relative to other recent periods. It is during these periods of relative trend strength. that the Mac-Stoch system works best. You are better off, therefore, looking for an hourly chart with long bars in the current period than short ones. This also gives you the advantage of not having to worry overly much about an unexpected, intraday change in Histogram direction.

5. FINAL WORD

A Final Word

You have in your hands an account of everything you need to know to execute profitable day-trades. But what is not in this Manual is perhaps the most important part of trading: **_real-time, real-money experience!_** There is no substitute for the countless hours it will take to put this knowledge into practice in a way that will lead you to find technically sound trading setups, make consistently profitable trades, take reasonably small losses, and ultimately ramp up your trading account to new highs. To put into practice what you have learned in this Manual, I suggest your taking the following steps:

- Read this Manual over at least twice. We all read through our prejudices, and these may cause you to overlook important bits of information. Go over and over this material to be sure to catch items you may have missed on the first reading.

- Spend several trading days just going over and over your watch lists. There is no substitute for putting in hours of "eyeballing" charts for the above setups. You will need to so internalize these setups that they become second nature to you. You need to gain that intuitive sense for stocks that look somewhat like a particular setup, but which have other "issues" going on which likely would weigh against the setup; and that intuitive sense for a setup that is just so outrageously perfect that you can hardly wait to enter your position on the entry signal!

- Give serious thought to position sizing. I recommend dividing your account into equal monetary amounts and putting no more than that amount into each trade. When you are first starting out as an day-trader, you will want to go very lightly into your trades. You can increase your size as you gain more experience. It is also not a bad idea to scale back on size during a losing streak and increase in size during a winning streak. That may seem counterintuitive, but in the game of trading, losing tends to beget more losing, and winning more winning.

- Consider subscribing to one of the market letters at DrStoxx.com. Each issue of our Stock and ETF letters are full of great treading ideas and can help you streamline your stock-finding process greatly.

- HAVE FUN! If trading is stressful, makes you anxious, causes you to lose sleep at night, interferes with your relationships and/or work responsibilities, then you are *DOING SOMETHING WRONG!* Even if you are "trading for a living", you should always be "trading for life!" That is the DrStoxx.com motto, and one we stand behind fully.

The last word by way of a disclaimer: short term trading of the type described in this Trading Manual is financially risky. Large amounts of money can be lost while implementing the strategies mentioned above. Readers of this Trading Manual assume all risks involved in trading this strategy, and will not hold Befriend the Trend Trading, LLC, in any way liable for any losses that may be incurred.

No portion of the above Trading Manual may be republished, retransmitted or forwarded without express written consent from Dr. Stoxx (Dr. Thomas K. Carr) and Befriend the Trend Trading, LLC.

Made in the USA
Charleston, SC
11 May 2016